ENCOUNTER . . .

ENCOUNTER . . .

WORD POWER

TODD SMITH

Printed by Pathway Press

ISBN: 978-087148-894-7

Dedication

I am thrilled to dedicate this book to the two most precious jewels in my life, my boys Ty and Ethan.

Words cannot come close to describing how I feel about you guys. You are awesome!

My prayer is that you will always have sweet memories of the times we spent together, the way I talked to you and the way I touched you.

I have tried hard to be what you needed, please forgive me for falling so short—Lets always be the best of friends—Love, DAD!

Introduction

Do you know that words have the power to change the world? Think about it. Wars are started and ended with words. Homes break-up or are peaceful because of words. Feelings are hurt because of words. Self esteem is solidified or destroyed because of words.

Words influence, however, no one's words have greater strength and power than GOD'S WORD.

John Mason said, "All mankind is divided into three classes: 1) those who are unchangeable, 2) those who are changeable, and 3) those who cause change. It is my desire that the scriptures you encounter and the quotes you read in this book will motivate you to CAUSE CHANGE!

WORD POWER was compiled to help you live a power filled life. Share it with a friend, a family member, and the world and see what happens!

Contents

Anxiety

Anxiety does not empty tomorrow of its sorrows but only empties today of its strength.

CHARLES HADDON SPURGEON (1834–1892)

- Casting the whole of your care, [all of your anxieties, all of your worries, all your concerns, once and for all]on Him, for He cares for you affectionately and cares about you watchfully. 1 Peter 5:7 (Amplified)

- Cast your burden on the Lord [releasing the weight of it] and He will sustain you; He will never allow the [consistently] righteous to be moved (made to slip, fall, or fail). Psalm 55:22 (Amplified)

- Look at the birds of the air, for they neither sow nor reap nor gather into barns; yet your heavenly Father feeds them. Are you not of more value than they? Matthew 6:26

Lord Jesus, make my heart sit down

AFRICAN PROVERB

- Do not be anxious about anything, but in everything, by prayer and petition, with thanksgiving, present your requests to God. Philippians 4:6 (NIV)

- And we know that all that happens to us is working for our good if we love God and are fitting into his plans. Romans 8:28 (LB)

Anxiety is the natural result when our hopes are centered in anything short of God and his will for us.

BILLY GRAHAM

- Rest in the LORD, and wait patiently for Him . . . Do not fret—it only causes harm. Psalm 37:7,8

- God is our refuge and strength, a very present help in trouble. Therefore we will not fear, even though the earth be removed, and though the mountains be carried into the midst of the sea; though its waters roar and be troubled, though the mountains shake with its swelling. Psalm 46:1-3

- Lord GOD, you have begun to show me, your servant, how great you are. You have great strength, and no other god in heaven or on earth can do the powerful things you do. There is no other god like you. Deuteronomy 3:24 (NCV)

The beginning of anxiety is the end of faith; and the beginning of true faith is the end of anxiety.

GEORGE MULLER (1805-1898)

- For I know the plans I have for you, declares the LORD, plans to prosper you and not to harm you, plans to give you hope and a future. Jeremiah 29:11 (NIV)
- Surely God is my salvation; I will trust and not be afraid. The LORD, the LORD, is my strength and my song; he has become my salvation. Isaiah 12:2 (NIV)

Anxiety is the interest paid on trouble before it is due.

WILLIAM RALPH INGE (1860-1954)

Baptism with the Holy Spirit

God commands us to be filled with the Spirit, and if we are not filled, it's because we are living beneath our privileges.

DWIGHT L. MOODY (1837–1899)

- I indeed baptize you with water unto repentance, but He who is coming after me is mightier than I, whose sandals I am not worthy to carry. He will baptize you with the Holy Spirit and fire. Matthew 3:11

- Jesus said, "If you then, being evil, know how to give good gifts to your children, how much more will your heavenly Father give the Holy Spirit to those who ask Him!" Luke 11:13

Before we can be filled with the Spirit, the desire to be filled must be all consuming. It must be for the time the biggest thing in the life, so acute, so intrusive as to crowd out everything else.

A.W. TOZER (1897–1963)

- Jesus said, "He who believes in Me, as the Scripture has said, out of his heart will flow rivers of living water." But this He spoke concerning the Spirit, whom those believing in

Him would receive; for the Holy Spirit was not yet given, because Jesus was not yet glorified. John 7:38,39

- Jesus said, "Peace to you! As the Father has sent Me, I also send you." And when He had said this, He breathed on them, and said to them, "Receive the Holy Spirit." John 20:22

If we seek the baptism of the Holy Ghost in order that God may make us great servants of his, we shall never receive anything. God baptizes us with the Holy Ghost that he may be all in all.

OSWALD CHAMBERS (1874–1917)

- Jesus said, "Behold, I send the Promise of My Father upon you; but tarry in the city of Jerusalem until you are endued with power from on high." Luke 24:49
- Jesus said, "For John truly baptized with water, but you shall be baptized with the Holy Spirit not may days from now." Acts 1:5
- Paul said, "Did you receive the Holy Spirit when you believed?" Acts 19:2
- Jesus said, "But you shall receive power when the Holy Spirit has come upon you; and you shall be witnesses to Me in Jerusalem, and in all Judea and Samaria, and to the end of the earth." Acts 1:8

Let no one pray for a mighty baptism of power who is not prepared for deep heart searchings and confession of sin.

EVAN ROBERTS

- And suddenly there came a sound from heaven, as of a rushing mighty wind, and it filled the whole house where they were sitting. Then there appeared to them divided tongues of fire, and one sat upon each of them. And they were all filled with the Holy Spirit and began to speak with other tongues, as the Spirit gave them utterance. Acts 2:2-4

- Now when the apostles . . . heard that Samaria had received the word of God, they sent Peter and John to them, who when they had come down, prayed for them that they might receive the Holy Spirit. For as yet He had fallen upon none of them. They had only been baptized in the name of the Lord Jesus. Then they laid hands on them, and they received the Holy Spirit. Acts 8:14-17

- And Ananias went his way and enter the house; and laying his hands on him he said, Brother Saul, the Lord Jesus, who appeared to you on the road as you came, has sent me that you may receive your sight and be filled with the Holy Spirit. Acts 9:17

The Holy Spirit descended upon me in a manner that seemed to go through me, body and soul. I could feel the impression like a wave of

electricity going through and through me. Indeed, it seemed to come in waves and waves of liquid love . . . like the very breath of God . . . it seemed to fan me like immense wings.

CHARLES G. FINNEY (1792–1875)

- While Peter was still speaking these words, the Holy Spirit fell upon all those who heard the word. Acts 10:44

- Peter said, "And as I began to speak the Holy Spirit fell upon them, as upon us at the beginning. Then I remembered the word of the Lord, how He said, 'John indeed baptized with water, but you shall be baptized with the Holy Spirit.'" Acts 11:15,16

To the church, Pentecost brought light, power, joy. There came to each illumination of mind, assurance of heart, intensity of love, fullness of power, exuberance of joy. No one needed to ask if they had received the Holy Ghost. Fire is self-evident. So is power!

SAMUEL CHADWICK (1832–1917)

- When they heard this, they were baptized in the name of the Lord Jesus. And when Paul had laid hands on them, the Holy Spirit came upon them, and they spoke with tongues and prophesied. Acts 19:5,6

There is one thing we cannot imitate: we cannot imitate being full of the Holy Ghost.

OSWALD CHAMBERS (1874–1917)

Children

Children must be valued as our most priceless possession.

JAMES DOBSON

- All your children shall be taught by the Lord, and great shall be the peace of your children. Isaiah 54:13
- Children's children are the crown of old men, and the glory of children is their father. Proverbs 17:6
- Behold, children are a heritage from the Lord, the fruit of the womb is a reward. Psalm 127:3

Kids are not a short-term loan, they are a long-term investment!

- But Jesus said, "Let the little children come to Me, and do not forbid them; for of such is the kingdom of heaven." Matthew 19:14
- In the last days, God says, I will pour out my Spirit on all people. Your sons and daughters will prophesy, your young men will see visions . . . Acts 2:17 (NIV)
- If you fully obey the LORD your God and carefully follow all his commands I give you today, the LORD your God will set you high above all the nations on earth. All these blessings will come upon you and accompany you

if you obey the LORD your God: You will be blessed in the city and blessed in the country. The fruit of your womb will be blessed . . . Deuteronomy 28:1-4a (NIV)

- Jesus said, "And any of you who welcomes a little child like this because you are mine is welcoming me and caring for me. But if any of you causes one of these little ones who trusts in me to lose faith, it would be better for you to have a rock tied to your neck and be thrown into the sea. Matthew 18:5,6 (LB)

If a child lives with criticism
he becomes a critic.

AUTHOR UNKNOWN

- Teach a child to choose the right path, and when he is older, he will remain upon it. Proverbs 22:6 (LB)

- And now a word to you parents. Don't keep on scolding and nagging your children, making them angry and resentful. Rather, bring them up with the loving discipline the Lord himself approves, with suggestions and godly advice. Ephesians 6:4 (LB)

Children have not been very good at listening to their elders, but they have never failed to imitate them.

JAMES BALDWIN

- Be kind to each other and be gentle. Forgive each other, just as God also forgave you through Christ. Ephesians 4:32
- This promise is for you, for your children, and for everyone who is far away. It is for all the people that the Lord our God will ask to come to Him. Acts 2:39

Childhood: that happy period when nightmares occur only during sleep.

Criticism

Do not remove a fly from your friend's forehead with a hatchet.

CHINESE PROVERB

- Therefore let us pursue the things which make for peace and the things by which one may edify another. Romans 4:19
- Therefore, comfort each other and edify one another . . .. 1 Thessalonians 5:11
- Let no corrupt word proceed out of your mouth, but what is good for necessary edification, that it may impart grace to the hearers. Ephesians 4:29
- Jesus said, "But I say unto you that for every idle word men may speak, they will give account of it in the day of judgment. For by your words you will be justified, and by your words you will be condemned." Matthew 12:36,37

He has the right to criticize who has the heart to help.

ABRAHAM LINCOLN (1809-1865)

- If I am able to speak the languages of people and of angels, but I do not have love for people, I am only like a noisy bell or a loud cymbal. Love is patient and kind. 1 Corinthians 13:1, 4

- Jesus said, "Why do you look at the small piece of dust that is in your brother's eye but you do not give attention to the large piece of wood in your eye? You are a hypocrite! Take out the large piece of wood from your eye first. Then you will see clearly to take out the small piece of dust from your brother's eye." Matthew 7:3,5

The Holy Ghost alone is in the true position of a critic; he is able to show what is wrong without wounding and hurting.

Oswald Chambers (1874-1917)

- For all the law is fulfilled in one word, even in this: "You shall love your neighbor as yourself." But if you bite and devour one another, beware lest you be consumed by one another! Galatians 5:14,15

- Let your speech always be with grace, seasoned with salt, that you may know how you ought to answer each one. Colossians 4:6

A sharp word cuts deeper than a weapon.

Proverb

- He who guards his mouth preserves his life, but he who opens wide his lips shall have destruction. Proverbs 13:3

- The tongue of the righteous is choice silver . . . the lips of the righteous feed many. Proverbs 10:20,21

Criticism, like rain, should be gentle enough to nourish a man's growth without destroying his roots.

FRANK A. CLARK

- Let all bitterness, wrath, anger, clamor, and evil speaking be put away from you with all malice, and be kind to one another, tender-hearted, forgiving one another, even as God in Christ forgave you. Ephesians 4:31,32

- Jesus said, "And just as you want men to do to you, you also do to them likewise. Luke 6:31

- Bless those who persecute you; bless and do not curse. Rejoice with those who rejoice, and weep with those who weep. Romans 12:14,15

- Jesus said, "Therefore be merciful, just as your Father also is merciful." Luke 6:36

To avoid criticism, do nothing, say nothing, be nothing.

ELBERT GREEN HUBBARD (1856-1915)

Death

All days travel toward death, the last one reaches it.

Michel Eyquem de Montaigne (1533-1592)

- Jesus said, "Let not your heart be troubled; you believe in God, believe also in Me. In My Father's house are many mansions; if it were not so, I would have told you. I go to prepare a place for you. And if I go and prepare a place for you, I will come again and receive you to Myself; that where I am, there you may be also." John 14:1-3

- Then I heard a voice from heaven say, "Write: 'Blessed are the dead who die in the Lord from now on.' 'Yes,' says the Spirit, 'they will rest from their labour, for their deeds will follow them.'" Revelation 14:13

- The righteous has a refuge when he dies. Proverbs 14:32

A funeral among men is a wedding feast among the angels.

Kahlil Gibran (1883-1931)

- Eye has not seen, nor ear heard, nor have entered into the heart of man the things which God has prepared for those who love Him. 1 Corinthians 2:9

■ For I consider that the sufferings of this present time are not worthy to be compared with the glory which shall be revealed in us. Romans 8:18

■ Precious in the sight of the Lord is the death of His saints. Psalm 116:15

Lord, grant that my last hour may be my best hour.

OLD ENGLISH PRAYER

■ The time of my departure is at hand. I have fought the good fight of faith, I have finished the race, I have kept the faith. Finally, there is laid up for me a crown of righteousness, which the Lord, the righteous Judge, will give to me on that Day, and not to me only but also to all who have loved His appearing. 2 Timothy 4:6-8

■ And God will wipe away every tear from their eyes; there shall be no more death, nor sorrow, nor crying. There shall be no more pain, for the former things have passed away. Revelation 21:4

■ Beloved, now we are children of God; and it has not yet been revealed what we shall be, but we know that when He is revealed, we shall be like Him, for we shall see Him as he is. 1 John 3:2

- He shall swallow up death forever, and the Lord God will wipe away tears from all faces . . . .Isaiah 25:8

This world is the land of the dying; the next is the land of the living.

TRYON EDWARDS (1809-1894)

- So when this corruptible has put on incorruption, and this mortal has put on immortality, then shall be brought to pass the saying that is written: "Death is swallowed up in victory." 1 Corinthians 15:54

- And it is appointed for men to die once, but after this the judgment. Hebrews 9:27

Like as the waves make toward the pebbled shore, so do our minutes hasten to their end.

WILLIAM SHAKESPEARE (1564-1616)

- Jesus said, "I am the resurrection and the life. He who believes in Me, though he may die, he shall live. And whoever lives and believes in Me shall never die. Do you believe this?" John 11:25,26

- He who believes in the Son has everlasting life; and he who does not believe the Son shall not see life, but the wrath of God abides on him. John 3:36

- But I do not want you to be ignorant, brethren, concerning those who have fallen asleep, lest you sorrow as others who have no hope. For if we believe that Jesus died and rose again, even so God will bring with Him those who sleep in Jesus. 1 Thessalonians 4:13-14

No man ever repented of being a Christian on his deathbed.

Hannah More (1745-1833)

- For He Himself has said, "I will never leave you nor forsake you." Hebrews 13:5
- Be faithful until death, and I will give you the crown of life. Revelation 2:10

There is no death. Only a change of worlds.

Chief Seattle

Depression

- To console those who mourn in Zion, To give them beauty for ashes, The oil of joy for mourning, The garment of praise for the spirit of heaviness; That they may be called trees of righteousness, The planting of the LORD, that He may be glorified. Isaiah 61:3

- I waited patiently for the Lord; And He inclined to me, and heard my cry. He also brought me up out of a horrible pit, out of the miry clay and set my feet upon a rock, and established my steps. He has put a new song in my mouth . . .. Psalm 40:1-3

- I will lift up my eyes to the hills; From whence comes my help? My help comes from the LORD, who made heaven and earth. He will not allow your foot to be moved; He who keeps you will not slumber. Behold, He who keeps Israel shall neither slumber nor sleep. The LORD is your keeper; The LORD is your shade at your right hand. Psalm 121:1-5

- Trouble and anguish have overtaken me, yet your commandments are my delights. Psalm 119:143

- You are my hiding place; you shall preserve me from trouble; you shall surround me with songs of deliverance. Psalm 32:7

- Anxiety in the heart of man causes depression, but a good word makes it glad. Proverbs 12:25
- Commit your way to the Lord, trust also in Him, and He shall bring it to pass. Psalm 37:5
- He who dwells in the secret place of the Most High shall abide under the shadow of the Almighty. I will say of the Lord, "He is my refuge and my fortress; my God, in Him I will trust." Psalm 91:1,2
- A merry heart does good, like medicine, but a broken spirit dries the bones. Proverbs 17:22
- No evil shall befall you, nor shall any plague come near your dwelling; for He shall give His angels charge over you. To keep you in all your ways. Psalm 91:10,11
- Do not be afraid of sudden terror, nor of trouble from the wicked when it comes; for the Lord will be your confidence, and will keep your foot from being caught. Proverbs 3:25,26
- Casting the whole of your care, [all of your anxieties, all of your worries, all your concerns, once and for all]on Him, for He cares for you affectionately and cares about you watchfully. 1 Peter 5:7 (Amplified)

Failure

Big shots are only little shots that keep shooting.

CHRISTOPHER MORLEY

- If we confess our sins, He is faithful and just to forgive us our sins and to cleanse us from all unrighteousness. 1 John 1:9
- I can do all things through Christ who strengthens me. Philippians 4:13
- Brethren, I do not count myself to have apprehended; but one thing I do, forgetting those things which are behind and reaching forward to those things which are ahead. Philippians 3:13

You don't drown by falling in the water; you drown by staying there.

EDWIN LOUIS COLE

- Therefore we also since we are surrounded by so great a cloud of witnesses, let us lay aside every weight, and the sin which so easily ensnares us, and let us run with endurance the race that is set before us. Hebrews 12:1
- I have fought the good fight, I have finished the race, I have kept the faith. 2 Timothy 4:7

God chooses what we go through; we choose how we go through it.

JOHN MAXWELL

- And the Lord will make you the head and not the tail; you shall be above only, and not be beneath, if you heed the commandments of the LORD your God, which I command you today, and are careful to observe them. Deuteronomy 28:13

- I would have lost heart, unless I had believed that I would see the goodness of the Lord in the land of the living. Psalm 27:13

The past should be a springboard not a hammock.

EDMOND BURKE

- Jesus said, ". . .if you have faith as a mustard seed, you will say to this mountain, 'Move from here to there,' and it will move; and nothing will be impossible for you." Matthew 17:20
- Jesus said, ". . .lo, I am with you always, even to the end of the age." Matthew 28:20
- I have been crucified with Christ and I no longer live, but Christ lives in me. The life I live in the body, I live by faith in the Son of God, who loved me and gave himself for me. Galatians 2:20 (NIV)

In me is working a power stronger than every other power. The life that is in me is a thousand times bigger than I am outside.

SMITH WIGGLESWORTH

- . . . If God is for us, who can be against us? Romans 8:31

Faith

When you have faith in God, worry has to take its flight.

JACK COE

- Fight the good fight of faith, and remain strong in the everlasting life you were chosen for . . . 1 Timothy 6:12
- For we walk by faith, not by sight. 2 Corinthians 5:7
- Watch, stand fast in the faith, be brave, be strong. 1 Corinthians 16:13

Real faith believes God right to the end.

SMITH WIGGLESWORTH

- So then faith comes by hearing, and hearing by the word of God. Romans 10:17
- And the prayer of faith will save the sick man, and the Lord will raise him up. James 5:15 (RSV)
- The blind men came to Jesus . . .and He said to them, Do you believe that I am able to do this? They said to Him, "Yes, Lord." Then He touched their eyes, and said, "It will be done to you because of your faith."

Faith begins where the will of God is known.

F.F. BOSWORTH

- Jesus said, "Have faith in God." Mark 11:22

■ For whatever is born of God is victorious over the world; and this is the victory that conquers the world, even our faith. 1 John 5:4 (AMP)

With God all things are possible, and all things are possible to him who believeth, for faith makes room for God to work and thus release omnipotence.

LILIAN B. YEOMANS

■ Jesus said, "Everything is possible for him who believes." Mark 9:23 (NIV)

■ In this confidence let us hold on to the hope that we profess without the slightest hesitation—for he is utterly dependable. Hebrews 10:23 (Philips)

■ Jesus said, "Therefore I say to you, whatever things you ask when you pray, believe that receive them, and you will have them." Mark 11:24

You get faith by studying the Word. Study that Word until something in you "knows that you know" and that you do not just hope that you know.

CARRIE JUDD MONTGOMERY

■ For with the heart one believes unto righteousness, and with the mouth confession is made unto salvation. Romans 10:10

A spiritual law that few recognize is that our confession rules us. It is what we confess with

our lips that really dominates our inner being.

F.F. BOSWORTH

- But we have the same Spirit of faith [as the Psalmist] according as it has been written and is at present on record, I believed, wherefore I spoke. 2 Corinthians 4:13 (Wuest)

- Fool! When will you ever learn that "believing" is useless without doing what God wants you to? Faith that does not result in good deeds is not real faith. James 2:20 (LB)

It is when active faith dares to believe God to the point of action, that something has to happen.

KATHRYN KUHLMAN

- Now faith is the substance of things hoped for, the evidence of things not seen. Hebrews 11:1

- Commit your way to the LORD, Trust also in Him, and He will do it. Psalm 37:5 (NAS)

If you have worry, you don't have faith, and if you have faith, you don't have worry.

JACK COE

- Jesus said, "Did I not say to you that if you would believe you would see the glory of God." John 11:40

We tend to get what we expect.

NORMAN VINCENT PEALE

Faithfulness

What lies behind us and what lies before us are tiny matters compared to what lies within us.

RALPH WALDO EMERSON

- Oh, love the LORD . . .for the LORD preserves the faithful. Psalm 31:23
- Jesus said, ". . .Be faithful unto death and I will give you the crown of life." Revelation 2:10
- My eyes shall be on the faithful of the land, that they may dwell with me. Psalm 101:6

The ultimate measure of a man is not where he stands in moments of comfort and convenience, but where he stands at times of challenge and controversy.

MARTIN LUTHER KING, JR.

- For the eyes of the LORD run to and fro throughout the whole earth, to show Himself strong on behalf of those whose heart is loyal to Him. 2 Chronicles 16:9
- Jesus said, "No one, having put his hand to the plow, and looking back, is fit for the kingdom of God." Luke 9:62

By all means, don't say, "If I can;" say, "I will."

ABRAHAM LINCOLN

- But My servant Caleb, because he has a different spirit in him and has followed Me fully, I will bring into the land where he went, and his descendants shall inherit it. Numbers 14:24
- Choose for yourselves this day whom you will serve . . .but as for me and my house we will serve the LORD. Joshua 24:15

Never, never, never . . .give up.

WINSTON CHURCHILL

- A wicked messenger falls into trouble: but a faithful ambassador brings health. Proverbs 13:17
- Jesus said, "He who is faithful in what is least is faithful also in much." Luke 16:10

As you are faithful this one thing is certain, the Lord will show you great and mighty things that you know not now.

STANLEY FRODSHAM

- Jesus said, "Well done, good servant; because you were faithful in a very little, have authority over ten cities." Luke 19:17
- Jesus said, "If anyone desires to come after Me, let him deny himself, and take up his cross and follow me." Matthew 16:24
- Moreover it is required in stewards that one be found faithful. 1 Corinthians 4:2

In order for a church to prosper, she must obey Jesus' teaching in all things.

WILLIAM SEYMOUR

- And the things that you have heard from me among many witnesses, commit these to faithful men who will be able to teach others also. 2 Timothy 2:2
- A faithful man shall abound with blessings. Proverbs 28:20
- Looking unto Jesus, the author and finisher of our faith, who for the joy that was set before Him endured the cross, despising the shame and has sat down at the right hand of the throne of God. Hebrews 12:2

Push yourself again and again . . ..Don't give an inch until the final buzzer sounds.

LARRY BIRD

Forgiveness

If God forgives us, we must forgive ourselves. Otherwise it is almost like setting up ourselves as a higher tribunal than him.

C.S. LEWIS (1898-1963)

- He has not punished us as we deserve for all our sins, for his mercy toward those who fear and honor him is as great as the height of the heavens above the earth. He has removed our sins as far away from us as the east is from the west. Psalm 103:10-12 (LB)
- But if we confess our sins to him, he can be depended on to forgive us and to cleanse us from every wrong. And it is perfectly proper for God to do this for us because Christ died to wash away our sins. 1 John 1:9 (LB)
- For You, Lord, are good, and ready to forgive, And abundant in mercy to all those who call upon You. Psalm 86:5
- Lord, if you keep in mind our sins, then who can ever get an answer to his prayers? But you forgive! What an awesome thing this is! Psalm 130:3,4 (LB)
- Where is another God like you, who pardons the sins of the survivors among his people? You cannot stay angry with your people, for

you love to be merciful. Once again you will have compassion on us. You will tread our sins beneath your feet; you will throw them into the depths of the ocean! Micah 7:18,19 (LB)

If God were not willing to forgive sin, then heaven would be empty.

GERMAN PROVERB

- Jesus said, "Do not judge, and you will not be judged. Do not condemn, and you will not be condemned. Forgive, and you will be forgiven. Luke 6:37 (NIV)
- Jesus said, "You have heard that it was said, 'You shall love your neighbor and hate your enemy.' But I say to you, love your enemies, bless those who curse you, do good to those who hate you, and pray for those who spitefully use you and persecute you." Matthew 5:43,44

Forgiveness is the fragrance that the flower leaves on the heel of the one who crushed it.

MARK TWAIN (1835-1910)

- Jesus said, "And when you stand praying, if you hold anything against anyone, forgive him so that your Father in heaven may forgive you your sins. Mark 11:26 (NIV)
- Jesus said, "Moreover, if your brother sins against you, go and tell him his fault between you and him alone. If he hears you, you have

gained your brother . . ..Then Peter came to Him and said, 'Lord, how often shall my brother sin against me, and I forgive him? Up to seven times?' Jesus said to him, 'I do not say to you, up to seven times, but up to seventy times seven.'" Matthew 18:15,20,21

- You must make allowance for each other's faults and forgive the person who offends you. Remember, the Lord forgave you, so you must forgive others. Colossians 3:13 (NLT)

Forgiveness is not an occasional act, it is a permanent attitude.

MARTIN LUTHER KING, JR. (1929-1968)

- Be kind and loving to each other, and forgive each other just as God forgave you in Christ. Ephesians 4:32 (NCV)

When you forgive you in no way change the past—but you sure do change the future.

BERNARD MELTZER

- Jesus said, "But when you are praying, first forgive anyone you are holding a grudge against, so that your Father in heaven will forgive you your sins too." Mark 11:22 (LB)

The act of forgiveness takes us out of the mundane and puts us in touch with the holy.

DALE HANSON BOURKEY

Healing

Jesus can heal anything, anywhere, any time, and anybody. All you have to do is put your faith in Him.

JACK COE

- When the even was come, they brought unto Him many that were possessed with devils: and He cast out the spirits with his word, and healed all that were sick. Matthew 8:16
- He sends forth His word and heals them and rescues them from the pit and destruction. Psalm 107:20
- How God anointed Jesus of Nazareth with the Holy Ghost and with power: who went about doing good, and healing all that were oppressed of the devil; for God was with Him. Acts 10:38

There is no disease in God and there is none in heaven. Disease and health cannot come from the same source.

JOHN ALEXANDER DOWIE

- Who Himself bore our sins in His own body on the tree, that we, having died to sins, might live for righteousness—by whose stripes you were healed. 1 Peter 2:24
- And great multitudes came unto Him, having with them those that were lame, blind, dumb,

maimed, and many others and cast them down at Jesus' feet; and He healed them. Matthew 15:30

Just believe what God says that Jesus has done for you, body, soul, and spirit—think about it, talk about it, sing about it, shout about it, and the praise cure has begun.

LILIAN B. YEOMANS

- He Himself took our infirmities and bore our sicknesses. Matthew 8:17
- Jesus said to the centurion, "Go your way; and as you have believed, so let it be done for you." And his servant was healed that same hour. Matthew 8:13

The only limit to the power of God lies within the individual.

KATHRYN KUHLMAN

- Is anyone among you sick? Let him call for the elders of the church, and let them pray over him, anointing him with oil in the name of the Lord. And the prayer of faith will save the sick, and the Lord will raise him up.... James 5:14,15
- Jesus said, "The thief does not come except to steal, and to kill, and to destroy. I have come that they may have life, and that they may have it more abundantly. John 10:10

God delights to heal his people.
God can keep us well.

HOWARD CARTER

- Let us hold fast to the confession of our hope without wavering, for He who promised is faithful. Hebrews 10:23
- Bless the LORD, O my soul, and forget not all his benefits: who forgives all your iniquities, Who heals all your diseases. Psalm 103:2,3
- But He was wounded for our transgressions, He was bruised for our iniquities; the chastisement of our peace was upon Him, and by His stripes we are healed. Isaiah 53:5

If you are believing God for something, watch what comes out of your mouth. Keep confessing the Word of God, and God will honor His Word.

DODIE OSTEEN

- And the very God of peace sanctify you wholly; and I pray God your whole spirit and soul and body be preserved blameless unto the coming of our Lord Jesus Christ. 1 Thessalonians 5:23
- But, view of the promise of God, he wavered not through unbelief, but was made strong in faith, giving glory to God. Romans 4:20 (Worrell)

Holy Spirit

Every time we say, "I believe in the Holy Spirit," we mean that we believe that there is a living God able and willing to enter human personality and change it.

J.B. PHILLIPS (1906–1963)

- Jesus said, "And I will ask the Father, and He will give you another Counselor to be with you forever—the Spirit of truth . . .for He lives with you and will be in you." John 14:16,17 (NIV)

- Jesus said, "But when the Spirit of truth, comes, He will guide you into all truth. He will not speak on His own; He will speak only what He hears, and He will tell you what is yet to come." John 16:13 (NIV)

- Jesus said, "But whoever drinks the water I give him will never thirst. Indeed, the water I give him will become in him a spring of water welling up to eternal life." John 4:14 (NIV)

- Jesus said, "Nevertheless I tell you the truth. It is to your advantage that I go away; for if I do not go away, the Helper will not come to you; but if I depart, I will send Him to you." John 16:7

It is extraordinary how things fall off from a man like autumn leaves once he comes to the place where there is no rule but that of the personal domination of the Holy Spirit.

OSWALD CHAMBERS (1874–1917)

■ For the kingdom of God is not a matter of eating and drinking, but of righteousness, peace and joy in the Holy Spirit. Romans 14:17 (NIV)

■ Jesus said, "But the Helper, the Holy Spirit, whom the Father will send in My name, He will teach you all things, and bring to your remembrance all things that I said to you." John 14:26

Living one day in the Spirit is worth more than a thousand lived in the flesh.

RICHARD OWEN ROBERTS

■ We have not received the spirit of the world but the Spirit who is from God, that we may understand what God has freely given us. 1 Corinthians 2:12 (NIV)

■ But if the Spirit of Him who raised Jesus from the dead dwells in you, He who raised Christ from the dead will also give life to your mortal bodies through His Spirit who dwells in you. Romans 8:11

The Spirit's control will replace sin's control. His power is greater than the power of all your sin.

ERWIN W. LUTZER

■ Or do you not know that your body is the temple of the Holy Spirit who is in you, whom you have from God, and you are not your own? 1 Corinthians 6:19

- For you did not receive the spirit that makes you a slave again to fear, but you received the Spirit of sonship. And by him we cry, "Abba, Father. Romans 8:15 (NIV)
- Be filled with the Holy Spirit. Ephesians 5:18
- Likewise the Spirit also helps in our weaknesses. For we do not know what we should pray for as we ought, but the Spirit Himself makes intercession for us with groanings which cannot be uttered. Romans 8:26

The anointing of the Holy Spirit is given to illuminate His Word, to open the Scriptures, and to place the spiritual man in direct communication with the mind of God.

CHARLES F. PARHAM

- For as many are led by the Spirit of God, these are the sons of God. Romans 8:14
- For my speech and my preaching were not with persuasive words of human wisdom; but in demonstration of the Spirit and of power—that your faith should not be in the wisdom of men but in the power of God. 1 Corinthians 2:4, 5

Leadership

**The moment you stop learning,
you stop leading.**

RICK WARREN

- Jesus said, "Yet it shall not be so among you; but whoever desires to become great among you, let him be your servant. And whoever desires to be first among you, let him be your slave." Matthew 20:26,27

- Shepherd the flock of God which is among you, serving as overseers, not by compulsion but willingly, not for dishonest gain but eagerly; nor as being lords over those entrusted to you, but being examples to the flock. 1 Peter 5:2,3

I start with the premise that the function of leadership is to produce more leaders, not more followers.

RALPH NADER

- Jesus said, "Can the blind lead the blind? Will they not both fall into the ditch?" Luke 6:39

Eagles don't flock—you have to find them one at a time.

H. ROSS PEROT

- No one engaged in warfare entangles himself with the affairs of this life, that he may please him who enlisted him as a soldier. 2 Timothy 2:4
- Jesus said, "A disciple is not above his teacher, but everyone who is perfectly trained will be like his teacher." Luke 6:40
- Look unto Jesus the author and finisher of our faith, who for the joy that was set before Him endured the cross, despising the shame, and has sat down at the right hand of the throne of God. Hebrews 12:2

Being in power is like being a lady. If you have to tell people you are, you aren't.

MARGARET THATCHER

- Only be strong and very courageous, that you may observe to do according to all the law which Moses My servant commanded you; do not turn from it to the right hand or to the left, that you may prosper wherever you go. Joshua 1:8
- In all your ways acknowledge Him, and He shall direct your paths. Proverbs 3:6

He who has learned to obey will know how to command.

SOLON (630 B.C.–560 B.C.)

- Commit your works to the Lord, and your thoughts will be established. Probverbs 16:3

- Never be lazy in your work, but serve the Lord enthusiastically. Romans 12:11 (LB)

Do not follow where the path may lead.
Go instead where there is
no path and leave a trail.

AUTHOR UNKNOWN

- Not that I have already attained, or am already perfected; but I press on, that I may lay hold of that for which Christ Jesus has also laid hold of me. Philippians 3:12

The ultimate leader is one who is willing to develop people to the point that they eventually surpass him or her in knowledge and ability.

FRED A. MANSKE, JR

- Set your mind on things above, not on things on the earth. Colossians 3:2

- Let your speech always be with grace, seasoned with salt, that you may know how you ought to answer each one. Colossians 4:6

Use power to help people. For we are given power not to advance our own purposes nor to make a great show in the world, nor a name. There is but one just use of power and it is to serve people.

GEORGE BUSH

Love

The biggest disease today is not leprosy or tuberculosis, but rather the feeling of being unwanted, uncared for, and deserted by everybody.

MOTHER TERESA

■ Whoever loves his brother lives in the light, and there is nothing in him to make him stumble. 1 John 2:10 (NIV)

■ Jesus said, "A new command I give you: Love one another, as I have loved you, so you must love one another." John 13:34 (NIV)

■ Dear friends, since God so loved us, we also ought to love one another. 1 John 4:11 (NIV)

I will not permit any man to narrow and degrade my soul by making me hate him.

BOOKER T. WASHINGTON

■ But above all these things put on love, which is the bond of perfection. Colossians 3:14

■ Jesus said, "All men will know that you are my disciples if you love one another. John 13:35 (NIV)

Hurting people hurt people.

JOHN MAXWELL

If you are going to play together as a team, you've got to care for one another. You've got to love each other.

VINCE LOMBARDI

- Two are better than one, because they have a good return for their work: If one falls down, his friend can help him up. But pity the man who falls and has no one to help him up! Ecclesiastes 4:9,10 (NIV)
- Jesus said, "Do to others as you would have them do to you." Luke 6:31
- Jesus said, "Greater love has no one than this, than to lay down one's life for his friends." John 15:13
- Let love be your greatest aim. 1 Corinthians 14:1

Love is my decision to make your problem my problem.

ROBERT SCHULLER

- And now abide faith, hope, love, these three; but the greatest of these is love. 1 Corinthians 13:13
- Let us not love in word or in tongue, but in deed and in truth. 1 John 3:18
- Love is very patient and kind, never jealous or envious, never boastful or proud, never haughty or selfish or rude. Love does not demand its own way. It is not irritable or touchy. It does not hold grudges and will hardly even notice when others do it wrong. 1 Corinthians 13:4,5 (LB)

- Love must be sincere. Hate what is evil; cling to what is good. Be devoted to one another in brotherly love. Honor one another above yourselves. Romans 12:9,10 (NIV)

- Now that you have purified yourselves by obeying the truth so that you have sincere love for your brothers, love one another deeply, from the heart. 1 Peter 1:22 (NIV)

To handle yourself, use your head. To handle others, use your heart.

JOHN MAXWELL

- Love . . .it is never glad about injustice, but rejoices whenever truth wins out. If you love someone, you will be loyal to him no matter what the cost. You will always believe in him, always expect the best of him, and always stand your ground in defending him. 1 Corinthians 13:6,7 (LB)

Plant a word of love heart-deep in a person's life. Nurture it with a smile and a prayer, and watch what happens.

MAX LUCADO

- Jesus said, "Love your enemies . . ." Matthew 5:44

Marriage

A happy marriage is the union of two good forgivers.

ROBERT QUILLEN (1887-1948)

- The man said, "This is now bone of my bones, and flesh of my flesh." Genesis 2:23 (NASB)
- A man will leave his father and mother for this reason, and be joined to his wife, and the two of them will become one body. This mystery is great . . .But each person among you must love his wife as much as he loves himself, and the wife must respect her husband. Ephesians 5:31,32,35
- The man who finds a wife finds a good thing; she is a blessing to him from the Lord. Proverbs 18:22 (LB)

The Christian is supposed to love his neighbor, and since his wife is his nearest neighbor, she should be his deepest love.

MARTIN LUTHER (1483-1546)

- Wives, let yourselves be under your husbands' authority because this is what the Lord wants you to do. Husbands, love your wives and be gentle with them. Colossians 3:18, 19
- Love your wives, just as Christ also loved the church and gave Himself for her . . .So hus-

bands should also love their wives like their own bodies. The man who loves his wife loves himself. Ephesians 5:25,28,29

A marriage is like a long trip in a tiny rowboat: if one passenger starts to rock the boat, the other has to steady it; otherwise they will go to the bottom together.

DAVID ROBERT REUBEN

■ Be tenderhearted, kind, humble, gentle, patient; bear with one another and forgive one another . . .as the Lord forgave you. With all this have love, which binds it all together. Colossians 3:12-14

Marriage is heaven or hell.

GERMAN PROVERB

■ You cover the altar of the Lord with tears . . . because He does not regard your offering any more . . .Yet you say, "Why?" It is because the Lord has been the witness between you and the wife of your youth, to whom you have been untrue, though she is your partner, and the wife you have promised to care for. Did the Lord not make them one? . . .Therefore guard you spirit, and let no one deal treacherously with the wife of his youth. "For I hate this putting away of a wife," says the Lord. You have wearied the Lord with your words. Malachi 2:12-17

■ Live happily with the woman you love through the fleeting days of life, for the wife God gives you is your best reward down here for all your earthly toil. Ecclesiastes 9:9

Success in marriage is more than finding the right person: it is being the right person.

Robert Browning (1812-1889)

Parenting

By the time we realize that our parents may have been right, we usually have children who think we are wrong.

AUTHOR UNKNOWN

- . . . we will tell the next generation the praiseworthy deeds of the LORD, his power, and the wonders he has done. Psalm 78:4 (NIV)

- And all thy children shall be taught of the LORD; and great shall be the peace of thy children. Isaiah 54:13

Every mother is like Moses. She does not enter the promised land. She prepares a world she will not see.

POPE PAUL VI

- Fathers, do not exasperate your children, instead, bring them up in the training and instruction of the LORD. Ephesians 6:4

- As for me and my house, we will serve the Lord. Joshua 24:15

- And these words, which I command you this day, shall be in your heart: And you shall teach them diligently unto your children, and shall talk of them when you sit in your house, and when you walk by the way, and when you lie down, and when you rise up. Deuteronomy 6:6, 7

The best gift a father can give to his son is the gift of himself—time.

C. NEIL STRAIT

- Fathers, do not embitter your children, or they will become discouraged. Colossians 3:21 (NIV)

- For I have chosen him, so that he will direct his children and his household after him to keep the way of the LORD by doing what is right. Genesis 18:19 (NIV)

The most important thing a father can do for his children is to love their mother.

THEODORE M. HESBURGH

- Children are a gift from the Lord. Babies are a reward. Psalm 127:3 (ICB)

Other things may change us, but we start and end with family.

ANTHONY BRANDT

- Train a child how to live the right way. Then even when he is old, he will still live that way. Proverbs 22:6 (ICB)

The most successful parents are those who have the skill to get behind the eyes of the child, seeing what he sees, thinking what he thinks, feeling what he feels.

JAMES C. DOBSON

■ An old man's grandchildren are his crowning glory. A child's glory is his father. Proverbs 17:6 (LB)

Build me a son, O Lord, who will be strong enough to know when he is weak and brave enough to face himself when he is afraid, one who will be proud and unbending in honest defeat, and humble and gentle in victory.

PRAYER OF DOUGLAS MACARTHUR

■ If you refuse to discipline your son, it proves you don't love him, for if you love him, you will be prompt to punish him. Proverbs 13:24

If it was going to be easy to raise kids, it never would have started with something called labor.

AUTHOR UNKNOWN

■ Like arrows in the hand of a warrior, so are the children of one's youth. Psalm 127:4

■ Teach them [the Word] to your children, talking about them when you sit at home and when you walk along the road, when you lie down and when you get up. Deuteronomy 11:19

Three things your kids will never forget about you: the TIME you spent with them, the way you TALKED to them, and the way you TOUCHED them.

TODD SMITH

Perseverance

When you are at the end of your rope . . .tie a knot and hang on.

FRANKLIN D. ROOSEVELT

- Let us not become weary in doing good, for at the proper time we will reap a harvest if we do not give up. Galatians 6:9 (NIV)

- You need to persevere so that when you have done the will of God, you will receive what he has promised. Hebrews 10:36 (NIV)

By perseverance the snail reached the ark.

CHARLES H. SPURGEON

- And we desire that each one of you show that same diligence to the full assurance of hope until the end, that you do not become sluggish, but imitate those who through faith and patience inherit the promises. Hebrews 6:11,12

- Not only so, but we also rejoice in our sufferings, because we know that suffering produces perseverance; perseverance, character; and character, hope. Romans 5:3,4

The nose of the bulldog is slanted backwards so he can continue to breathe without letting go.

WINSTON CHURCHILL

- Therefore . . .be steadfast, immovable, always abounding in the work of the Lord, knowing that your labor is not in vain in the Lord. 1 Corinthians 15:58
- Therefore . . .be diligent to be found by Him in peace, without spot and blameless. 2 Peter 3:14

Following the path of least resistance is what makes men and rivers crooked.

LARRY BIELAT

- Do you see a man who excels in his work? He will stand before kings . . . Proverbs 22:29
- Consider it pure joy, my brothers, whenever you face trials of many kinds, because you know that the testing of your faith develops perseverance. Perseverance must finish its work so that you may be mature and complete, not lacking anything. James 1:2-4 (NIV)
- Let us hold unswervingly to the hope we profess, for He who promised is faithful. Hebrews 10:23 (NIV)

The human spirit is never finished when it is defeated . . . it is finished when it surrenders.

BEN STEIN

- You therefore must endure hardship as a good soldier of Jesus Christ. 2 Timothy 2:3

It's not where you start—It's where you finish that counts.

ZIG ZIGLAR

- Fight the good fight of faith, lay hold on eternal life, to which you were also called and have confessed the good confession in the presence of many witnesses. 1 Timothy 6:12

Of all sad words of tongue or pen, the saddest are these: "It might have been!"

JOHN GREENLEAF WHITTIER

- These troubles and sufferings of ours are, after all, quite small and won't last very long. Yet this short time of distress will result in God's richest blessing upon us forever and ever! 2 Corinthians 4:17 (LB)

The most pathetic person in the world is someone who has sight but has not vision.

HELEN KELLER

- For I consider that the sufferings of this present time are not worthy to be compared with the glory which shall be revealed in us. Romans 8:18

- If you faint in the day of adversity, your strength is small. Proverbs 24:10

Prayer

Real prayer—determined, prevailing prayer—is the greatest outlet of power on earth.

A.A. ALLEN

- Jesus said, "Therefore I say to you, whatever things you ask when you pray, believe that you receive them, and you will have them." Mark 11:24

- Jesus said, "Again I say to you that if two of you agree on earth concerning anything that they ask, it will be done for them by My Father in heaven." Matthew 18:19

All He [God] asks for is that simplicity of faith which will take Him at His Word.

JAMES SALTER

- Call to Me, and I will answer you, and show you great and mighty things, which you do not know. Jeremiah 33:3

- O' Lord, hear me praying...each morning I will look to You in heaven and lay my requests before You, praying earnestly. Psalm 5:1,3 (LB)

- Jesus said, "If you abide in Me, and My words abide in you, you will ask what you desire, and it shall be done for you." John 15:7

Seeing only what God says will produce and increase faith. Don't doubt your faith, doubt your doubts for they are unreliable.

F.F. BOSWORTH

- Jesus said, "Ask, and it will be given to you; seek, and you will find; knock it will be opened to you. For everyone who asks receives, and he who seeks finds, and to him who knocks it will be opened." Matthew 7:7,8

- Now this is the confidence that we have in Him. That if we ask anything according to His will, He hears us. And if we know that He hears us, whatever we ask, we know that we have the petitions that we have asked of Him. 1 John 5:14,15

- Jesus said, "And whenever you stand praying, if you have anything against anyone, forgive him, that your Father in heaven may also forgive you your trespasses." Mark 11:25

Prayer and prayer alone, much prayer, persistent prayer, is the door of entrance into the heart of God.

JOHN G. LAKE

- And when they had prayed, the place where they were assembled together was shaken; and they were all filled with the Holy Spirit, and they spoke the word of God with boldness. Acts 4:31

When you are in trouble, go to the throne before you go to the phone.

JOYCE MEYER

- Let us therefore come boldly to the throne of grace, that we may obtain mercy and find grace to help in time of need. Hebrews 4:16
- But you, beloved, building yourselves up on your most holy faith, praying in the Holy Spirit. Jude 20
- I love the Lord, because He has heard my voice and my supplications. Because He has inclined His ear to me, therefore I will call upon Him as long as I live. Psalm 116:1,2
- It shall come to pass that before they call, I will answer; and while they are still speaking, I will hear. Isaiah 65:24

A man without prayer is like a tree without roots.

POPE PIUS XII (1876-1958)

As artists give themselves to their models, and poets to their classical pursuits, so must we addict ourselves to prayer.

CHARLES H. SPURGEON (1834-1892)

- Then you shall call, and the Lord will answer; you shall cry, and He will say, "Here I am." Isaiah 58:9

■ Blessed be God, who has not turned away my prayer, nor His mercy from me. Psalm 66:20

Don't expect a thousand-dollar answer to a ten-cent prayer.

AUTHOR UNKNOWN

■ Be anxious for nothing, but in everything by prayer and supplication, with thanksgiving, let your requests be made known to God; and the peace of God which surpasses all understanding, will guard your hearts and minds through Christ Jesus. Philippians 4:6,7

If you can beat the devil in the matter of regular daily prayer, you can beat him anywhere. If he can beat you there, he can possibly beat you anywhere.

PAUL DANIEL RADER (1879-1938)

■ Likewise the Spirit also helps in our weaknesses. For we do not know what we should pray for as we ought, but the Spirit Himself makes intercession for us with groanings which cannot be uttered. Romans 8:26

Don't pray when you feel like it. Have an appointment with the Lord and keep it. A man is powerful on his knees.

CORRIE TEN BOOM (1892-1983)

Salvation

If any man wills to be a Christian, he can be a Christian. If you go to hell you go of your own accord.

AIMEE SEMPLE McPHERSON

- For this is good and acceptable in the sight of God our Saviour; who desires all men to be saved and to come to the knowledge of the truth. 1 Timothy 2:3,4
- For all have sinned and fall short of the glory of God. Romans 3:23
- There is none righteous, no, not one. Romans 3:10

I remember two things: that I am a great sinner and that Christ is a great Savior.

JOHN NEWTON (1725–1807)

- For the wages of sin is death, but the gift of God is eternal life in Christ Jesus our Lord. Romans 6:23
- Yes, Adam's sin brought punishment to all, but Christ's righteousness makes men right with God, so that they can live. Romans 5:18 (LB)

It is not your hold of Christ that saves you, but his hold of you!

CHARLES H. SPURGEON

- But God demonstrates His own love toward us, in that while we were still sinners, Christ died for us. Romans 5:8
- Therefore, just as through one man sin entered the world, and death through sin, and thus death spread to all men, because all sinned. Romans 5:12
- For whosoever calls on the name of the LORD shall be saved. Romans 10:13

God does not patch up the old life, or make certain repairs on the life;
He gives a new life, through the new birth.

KATHRYN KUHLMAN

- Jesus said, "Unless one is born again, he cannot see the kingdom of God." John 3:3
- For God did not send His Son into the world to condemn the world, but that the world through Him might be saved. John 3:17

The knowledge of sin is the beginning of salvation.

EPICURUS (341–270 B.C.)

- For by grace you have been saved through faith, and that not of yourselves; it is the gift of God, not of works, lest anyone should boast. Ephesians 2:8,9
- If we confess our sins, He is faithful and just to forgive us our sins and to cleanse us from all unrighteousness. 1 John 1:9

■ Come now, and let us reason together, says the LORD, though your sins are like scarlet, they shall be as white as snow; though they are red like crimson, they shall be as wool. Isaiah 1:18

■ Oh, taste and see that the LORD is good; blessed is the man who trusts in Him! Psalm 34:8

■ Jesus said, "Come, follow me!" Luke 18:22

■ And he brought them out and said, "Sirs, what must I do to be saved?" So they said, "Believe on the Lord Jesus Christ, and you will be saved, you and your household." Acts 16:31

God proved his love on the cross.
When Christ hung, and bled, and died,
it was God saying to the world,
"I love you."

BILLY GRAHAM

■ Therefore, if anyone is in Christ, he is a new creation; old things have passed away; behold, all things have become new. 2 Corinthians 5:17

We ain't what we want to be.
We ain't what we gonna be.
But thank God, we ain't what we was.

MARTIN LUTHER KING, JR. (1929-1968)

■ Jesus said, "For God so loved the world that He gave His only begotten Son, that whoever believes in Him should not perish but have everlasting life. John 3:16

Spirit of Excellence

Always do more than is required of you.

GENERAL GEORGE S. PATTON

- But My servant Caleb, because he has a different spirit in him and has followed Me fully, I will bring into the land where he went, and his descendants shall inherit it. Numbers 14:24
- "Be strong and work," says the Lord of hosts, "for I am with you." Haggai 2:4
- The lazy man desires much, and has nothing, but ... the diligent shall prosper. Proverbs 13:4
- Whatever your hand finds to do, do it with all your strength. Ecclesiastes 9:10

True greatness consists in being great in little things.

CHARLES SIMMONS

- The Lord shall bless you in all your works, and in all you put your hand to. Deuteronomy 15:10
- We must do the work of the One who sent Me while it is day. Night is coming, and no one can work then. John 9:4

Excellence is the result of caring more than others think is wise; risking more than oth-

ers think is safe; dreaming more than others thinks is practical and expecting more than others think is possible.

AUTHOR UNKNOWN

■ Whatever you do or say, do it all in the name of the Lord Jesus. Colossians 3:17

Choose to do what you can do, and God will help you do what you cannot do.

JOYCE MEYER

■ I have filled him with the Spirit of God, with skill, ability and knowledge in all kinds of crafts. Exodus 31:3 (NIV)

■ If any man minister, let him do it as of the ability which God supplies, that in all things God may be glorified through Jesus Christ, to whom belong the glory and dominion forever and ever. 1 Peter 4:11

Winners concentrate on winning; losers concentrate on getting by.

JOHN MAXWELL

■ Do not neglect the gift that is in you.... 1 Timothy 4:14

■ We want each of you to try hard...in your service and work until the end, so you can be sure of your hope. Don't be lazy but be like the people who inherit God's promises through faith and patience. Hebrews 6:11,12

Ability is what you're capable of doing.
Motivation determines what you do.
Attitude determines how well you do it.

LOU HOLTZ

Success

Nothing gives one person so much advantage over another as to remain always cool and unruffled under all circumstances.

THOMAS JEFFERSON

- That everyone may eat and drink, and find satisfaction in all his toil—this is the gift of God. Ecclesiastes 3:13 (NIV)
- Humility and the fear of the LORD bring wealth and honor and life. Proverbs 22:4 (NIV)
- The Lord your God will make you successful in everything you do...But you must obey the Lord your God. You must obey His commands and rules that are written in this Book of the Teachings. You must follow the Lord your God with your whole being. Deuteronomy 30:9,10 (ICB)
- Ponder the path of your feet, and let all your ways be established. Do not turn to the right or the left; remove your foot from evil. Proverbs 4:26,27

Consider the postage stamp. Its usefulness consists in the ability to stick to something until it gets there.

JOSH BILLINGS

- The house of the righteous contains great treasure, but the income of the wicked brings them trouble. Proverbs 15:6

- The LORD will make you the head, not the tail. If you pay attention to the commands of the LORD your God that I give you this day and carefully follow them, you will always be at the top, never at the bottom. Deuteronomy 28:11-13 (NIV)

Ninety-nine percent of failures come from people who have a habit of making excuses.

GEORGE WASHINGTON

- Happy are those who respect the LORD and obey Him. You will enjoy what you work for, and you will be blessed with good things. Psalm 128:1,2 (NCV)
- Blessed is the man...whose delight is in the law of the LORD, and in His law he meditates day and night. He shall be like a tree planted by the rivers of water, that brings forth its fruit in its season, whose leaf shall not wither; and whatever he does shall prosper. (Psalm 1:1-3)

Successful leaders have the courage to take action while others hesitate.

JOHN MAXWELL

- Commit your way to the Lord, trust also in Him, and He will do it. Psalm 37:5 (NAS)
- If you wait for perfect conditions, you will never get anything done...Keep on sowing your seed, for you never know which will grow—

perhaps it all will. Ecclesiastes 11:4,6 (LB)

- I will instruct you (says the Lord) and guide you along the best pathway for your life; I will advise you and watch your progress. Psalm 32:8 (LB)

- I can do all things through Christ who strengthens me. Philippians 4:13

A Recipe For Success:

Study while others are sleeping; work while others are loafing; prepare while others are playing and dream while others are wishing.

WILLIAM WARD

One who is contented with what he has done will never be famous for what he will do.

CHRISTIAN BOVEE

- For in Him (Jesus) we live and move and have our being. Acts 17:27 (NIV)

- I will instruct you and teach you in the way you should go; I will guide you with My eye. Psalm 32:8

You are the same today that you are going to be in five years from now except for two things: the people with whom you associate and the books you read.

CHARLES "TREMENDOUS" JONES

Tongue

The tongue is the ambassador of the heart.

JOHN LYLY (1554–1606)

- Jesus said, "For out of the abundance of the heart the mouth speaks." Matthew 12:34
- Let no corrupt word proceed out of your mouth, but what is good for necessary edification, that it may impart grace to the hearers. Ephesians 4:29
- A word fitly spoken is like apples of gold in settings of silver. Proverbs 25:11

A slip of the foot you may soon recover, but a slip of the tongue you may never get over.

BENJAMIN FRANKLIN

- Set a guard, O LORD, over my mouth; keep watch over the door of my lips. Psalm 141:3
- So then . . .let every man be swift to hear, slow to speak, slow to wrath. James 1:19
- Jesus said, "Every idle word men may speak, they will give account of it in the day of judgment." Matthew 12:36

If you are believing God for something, watch what comes out of your mouth. Keep on confessing the Word of God, and God will honor His Word.

DODIE OSTEEN

■ Jesus said, "Whoever says to this mountain, 'Be removed and be cast into the sea,' and does not doubt in his heart, but believes that those things he says will be done, he will have whatever he says." Mark 11:23

■ Keep your mouth closed and you will stay out of trouble. Proverbs 21:23 (LB)

You have not lived today until you have done something for someone who can never repay you.

JOHN BUNYAN

■ Pleasant words are like a honeycomb, sweetness to the soul and health to the bones. Proverbs 16:24

We set the atmosphere in the home, and we do that by taking the Word of God and praying and confessing it for our home.

MARILYN HICKEY

■ Don't talk so much. You keep putting your foot in your mouth. Be sensible and turn off the flow. Proverbs 10:19 (LB)

The man who knows most speaks least.

JEWISH PROVERB

■ Death and life are in the power of the tongue. Proverbs 18:21

Winning

I can expect failure, everyone fails at something. But I can't accept not trying.

MICHAEL JORDAN

Change your thoughts and you change your world.

NORMAN VINCENT PEALE

■ Fear not, for I am with you; be not dismayed, for I am your God. I will strengthen you, yes, I will help you, I will uphold you with My righteous right hand. Isaiah 41:10

■ To him who overcomes I will give to eat from the tree of life, which is in the midst of the Paradise of God. Revelation 2:7

Champions are a rare breed. They see beyond the dangers, the risks, the obstacles, and the hardships.

DR. LESTER SUMRALL

■ Dear young friends, you belong to God and have already won your fight with those who are against Christ because there is someone in your hearts who is stronger than any evil teacher in this wicked world. 1 John 4:4 (LB)

God created the world out of nothing, and as long as we are nothing, He can make something out of us.

MARTIN LUTHER

- Yet in all these things we are more than conquerors through Him who loved us. Romans 8:37
- Jesus said, "In this world you will have trouble. But take heart! I have overcome the world. John 16:33

Football games are generally won by the boys with the greatest desire.

PAUL "BEAR" BRYANT

- Don't let the world around you squeeze you into its own mold, but let God remake you so that your whole attitude of mind is changed. Romans 12:2 Phillips
- Jesus said, "For whoever desires to save his life will lose it, but whoever loses his life for My sake will find it." Matthew 16:25

No man could be ideally successful until he has found his place. Like a locomotive, he is strong on the track, but weak anywhere else.

ORSEN MARDEN

God chooses what we go through; we choose how we go through it.

JOHN MAXWELL

- And let us not get tired of doing what is right, for after a while we will reap a harvest of blessing if we don't get discouraged and give up. Galatians 6:9 (LB)
- In a race everyone runs, but only one person

gets first prize. So run your race to win. To win the contest you must deny yourselves many things that would keep you from doing your best. An athlete goes to all this trouble just to win a blue ribbon or a silver cup, but we do it for a heavenly reward that never disappears. 1 Corinthians 9:24,25 (LB)

■ Therefore, we also, since we are surrounded by so great a cloud of witnesses, let us lay aside every weight, and the sin which so easily ensnares us, and let us run with endurance the race that is set before us. Hebrews 12:1

You'll always have everything in life that you want, if you'll help enough other people get what they want.

ZIG ZIGLAR

■ Brethren, I do not count myself to have apprehended; but one thing I do, forgetting those things which are behind and reaching forward to those things which are ahead. I press toward the goal for the prize of the upward call of God in Christ Jesus. Philippians 3:13,14

The quality of a person's life is in direct proportion to their commitment to excellence, regardless of their chosen field of endeavor.

VINCE LOMBARDI

■ So I run straight to the goal with purpose in every step. I fight to win. I'm just not shadow boxing or playing around. 1 Corinthians 9:26 (LB)

Wisdom

Rule #1: Don't sweat the small stuff.
Rule #2: It's all small stuff.

DR. MICHAEL MANTELL

- Get wisdom! Get understanding! Proverbs 4:5
- Happy is the man who finds wisdom, and the man who gains understanding; for her proceeds are better than the profits of silver, and her gain than fine gold. Proverbs 3:13,14
- Wisdom is found on the lips of him who has understanding, but a rod is for the back of him who is devoid of understanding. Proverbs 10:13

A single conversation across the table with a wise man is worth a month's study of books.

PROVERB

- The fear of the LORD is the beginning of wisdom, and the knowledge of the Holy One is understanding. Proverbs 9:10
- To be wise is as good as being rich; in fact, it is better. You can get anything by either wisdom or money, but being wise has many advantages. Ecclesiastes 7:11,12 (LB)

It is better to weep with wise men than to laugh with fools.

SPANISH PROVERB

- And Jesus increased in wisdom and stature, and in favor with God and men. Luke 2:52
- Walk in wisdom toward those who are outside, redeeming the time. Colossians 4:5
- If you want to know what God wants you to do, ask Him, and He will gladly tell you, for He is always ready to give a bountiful supply of wisdom to all who ask Him; He will not resent it. James 1:5

As long as you're green, you're growing; as soon as you're ripe you start to rot.

RAY KROC

- He who wins souls is wise. Proverbs 11:30
- Do not be wise in your own eyes; fear the LORD and depart from evil. Proverbs 3:7

The art of being wise is the art of knowing what to overlook.

WILLIAM JAMES

- My son, pay attention to my wisdom; lend your ear to my understanding. Proverbs 5:1
- Wisdom is the principal thing; therefore get wisdom. And in all your getting get understanding. Proverbs 4:7

Word of God

A new world will arise out of the religious mists when we approach our Bible with the idea that it is . . . a Book which is now speaking.

A.W. TOZER (1897-1963)

- My son, give attention to My words; incline your ear to My sayings. Do not let them depart from your eyes; keep them in the midst of your heart. For they are life to those who find them, and health to all their flesh. Proverbs 4:20-22

- Jesus said, "Heaven and earth will pass away, but My words will by no means pass away. Luke 21:33

- God's word is alive and working. It is sharper than a sword sharpened on both sides. It cuts all the way into us, where the soul and spirit are joined. It cuts to the center of our joints and our bones. Hebrews 4:12 (ICB)

- The whole Bible was given to us by inspiration from God and is useful to teach us what is true and to make us realize what is wrong in our lives; it straightens us out and helps us do what is right. 2 Timothy 3:16 (LB)

When we pick up the Bible it would be good to remember that It is the Book with God in It; life in It; a God-indwelt Book.

E.W. KENYON

We are not walking in the Word if our thoughts are opposite of what it says. We are not walking in the Word if we are not thinking in the Word.

JOYCE MEYER

■ So shall My word be that goes forth from My mouth; it shall not return to Me void, but it shall accomplish what I please, and it shall prosper in the thing for which I sent it. Isaiah 55:11

■ Your word I have hidden in my heart, that I might not sin against You. Psalm 119:11

■ Then the LORD said to me, "You have seen well, for I am ready to perform My word." Jeremiah 1:12

God rejoices when we manifest a faith that holds Him to His Word.

SMITH WIGGLESWORTH

■ My son, do not forget my law, but let your heart keep My commands; for length of days and long life and peace they will add to you. Proverbs 3:1,2

■ Your word is a lamp to my feet and a light to my path. Psalm 119:105

Go all the way, don't let anything keep you from appropriating the promises of God in your life.

A.A. ALLEN

- My people are destroyed from lack of knowledge. "Because you have rejected knowledge, I also reject you as My priests; because you have ignored the law of your God, I also will ignore your children. Hosea 4:6 (NIV)
- So then faith comes by hearing and hearing by the word of God. Romans 10:17
- The entrance of Your words gives light; it gives understanding to the simple. Psalm 119:130
- Blessed is the man...who has his delight in the law of the LORD, and in His law he meditates day and night. He shall be like a tree planted by the rivers of water, that brings forth its fruit in its season, whose leaf also shall not wither; and whatever he does shall prosper. Psalm 1:1,2-4

A Bible that is falling a part probably belongs to someone who isn't.

CHRISTIAN JOHNSON

A thorough knowledge of the Bible is worth more than a college education.

THEODORE ROOSEVELT (1858-1919)

- Do what God's teachings say; do not just listen and do nothing. When you only sit and listen, you are only fooling yourselves. James 1:22